Pip, Jin and Slink are in the garden.

Thunder cracks in the air.
Jin frowns. "Did you hear that?"

Stuck
in the
Storm

by Becca Heddle
Illustrated by Bill Ledger

OXFORD

UNIVERSITY PRESS

In this story ...

Pip

Pip is strong. She has the power to lift rocks.

Jin

Slink

2

Pip groans. "We must get in now to avoid the storm."

They run as fast as they can.

All of a sudden, lightning hits
a big tree.

The tree crashes down.
They are stuck in the storm!

Pip is sure she can help.
"Stand clear! I will lift the tree."

Pip grabs the tree.
She starts to lift it up.

Her feet skid in the wet soil.

Pip digs her heels in to stop skidding.

She lifts the tree clear.

Just then, the sun appears.

Pip, Jin and Slink get towels and
hot drinks.

That is better!

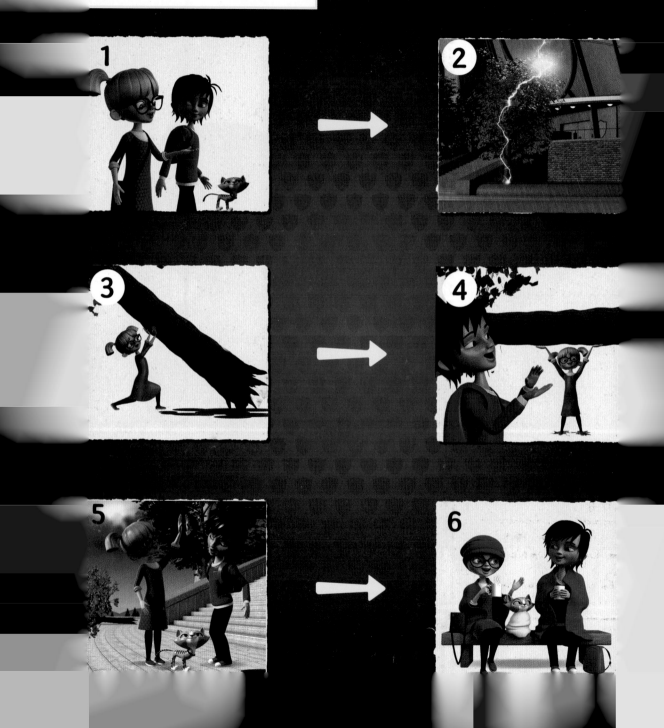